Bits in your Brain

Bits in Your Brain
Author: Dr. Danielle Marr
Illustration and Design: Felipe Matos
First published in the United Kingdom in 2025

Paperback ISBN: 978-1-7384370-1-6
Hardback ISBN: 978-1-7384370-2-3
Copyright © 2025 Dr Danielle Marr

All rights reserved. No part of this book may be reproduced, stored in a retrieval system, or transmitted in any form or by any means, electronic, mechanical, photocopying, recording, or otherwise, without the prior written permission of the publisher, except in the case of brief quotations embodied in critical articles or reviews.
The moral right of the author has been asserted.

This book is a work of fiction. While every effort has been made to ensure accuracy, the publisher and author accept no responsibility for errors or omissions, or for any loss or damage caused by reliance on the information contained within.

Any references to brands, organisations, or individuals are made in good faith and do not imply endorsement or affiliation. All trademarks and registered trademarks remain the property of their respective owners. Any similarity to persons living or dead is purely coincidental.

Bits in your Brain

Written by **Dr. Danielle Marr**

Illustratred by **Felipe Matos**

Dedicated to Stephen (Stessy Rouge) – D. M. ♥

You have bugs in your belly and bits in your brain –

this human body is really insane!

Let's talk about emotions, 'cause the fun ones are nice!
We love to feel good, but they come with a price.

Sometimes I'm grumpy, angry or mad — but to be honest, I'd rather feel glad.

We'd love these good feelings most of the time,
but they're not meant to turn on without reason or rhyme.

We can't always be happy — that's more than ok — but it helps to understand what makes us that way.

Taking care of our happiness is not what you think.
It's not in your toy box, it's not in your drink.

There are 4 tiny bits that help your brain feel good —
they are pretty big words, so listen up if you could!

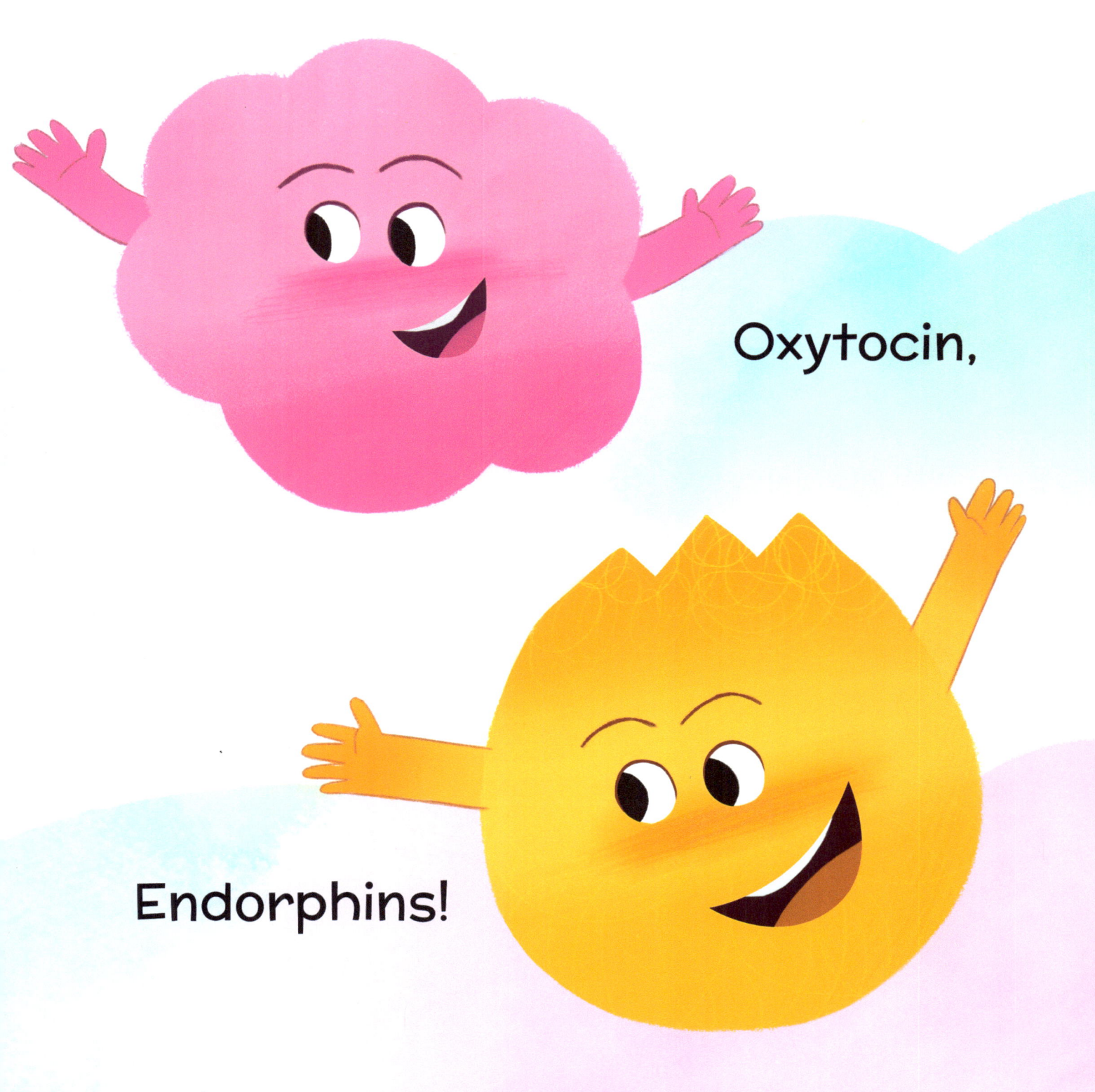

Oxytocin,

Endorphins!

Seratonin helps protect our good moods,
it helps us to sleep and comes from good foods.

Most of our serotonin is made in our gut,
but it works in our brain — I know!! Say whaaat?!

Feeling excited means dopamine's worked —
it's a chemical surge when pleasure is perked!

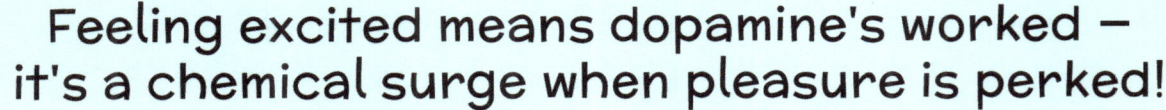

Dopamine makes us proud
when we've accomplished hard things —
that's why it's important to go chase your dreams!

It may be stolen by too much time on that screen!

Oxytocin makes us feel happy and loved –
we get little bits when we sneak in some hugs.

Cuddle your dog or hold your mom's hand –
being with people helps you feel grand.

Our brain releases endorphins when we exercise – get that heart rate up, I always advise!

Running and sweating makes us feel best — endorphins help us to manage our stress.

With sunshine, good sleep, and moving each day,
we help keep the worries and sadness away.

If you want to feel good, protect these 4 things — keep them in balance to enjoy what life brings.

Sometimes we're sad, angry or blue –

and that's ok, those feelings are true.

Even tough emotions have something to say –

they help us grow stronger in their own way.

A note from Dr. Marr:

Dear parents,
Sometimes we need to engage in activities that help us build up our supply of these "bits" in our brains. But in today's fast-paced world, where instant gratification is the norm, we must be mindful of the things that can drain them – high-sugar diets, overstimulation, overscheduling, and too much screentime, to name a few.

Thankfully, the things that build up and deplete our supply of these chemical messengers (the "bits") are quite similar across all four types.

Things that build our supplies:

- Quality Sleep
- Balanced Diet – High protein, healthy fat, healthy carbohydrates
- Daily exercise
- Sunlight
- Healthy relationships
- Gut health! (It's true! 90% of our body's serotonin is made in the gut!)

Things that deplete it:

- Too much screentime
- Instant gratification
- Sleep deprivation
- Chronic stress
- Poor/high processed/high sugar diets
- Social isolation

But, dear parents, what works for our kids, works for us adults, too!

www.ingramcontent.com/pod-product-compliance
Lightning Source LLC
Chambersburg PA
CBHW041107070526
44583CB00002B/99